Bridgestone
B O O K S

World of Reptiles

Komodo Dragons

by Jason Glaser

Consultant:
The Staff of the Reptile Gardens
Rapid City, South Dakota

Capstone
press

Bridgestone Books are published by Capstone Press,
151 Good Counsel Drive, P.O. Box 669, Mankato, Minnesota 56002.
www.capstonepress.com

Library of Congress Cataloging-in-Publication Data
Glaser, Jason.
    Komodo dragons / by Jason Glaser.
    p. cm.—(Bridgestone books. World of reptiles)
    Summary: "A brief introduction to Komodo dragons, discussing their characteristics,
range, habitat, food, offspring, and dangers. Includes a range map, life cycle diagram, and
amazing facts"—Provided by publisher.
    Includes bibliographical references (p. 23) and index.
    ISBN-13: 978-0-7368-5422-1 (hardcover)
    ISBN-10: 0-7368-5422-3 (hardcover)
    1. Komodo dragon—Juvenile literature. I. Title. II. World of reptiles.
QL666.L29G53   2006
597.95'968—dc22   2005020073

Editorial Credits

Christine Peterson, editor; Enoch Peterson, set designer; Kim Brown and Patrick Dentinger, book
    designers; Jo Miller, photo researcher; Scott Thoms, photo editor; Tami Collins, illustrator;
    Nancy Steers, map illustrator

Photo Credits

Corbis/Stuart Westmorland, 18
Getty Images Inc./ Steve Finn, 4
Minden Pictures/Tui De Roy, 10
Nature Picture Library/Michael Pitts, 12
Peter Arnold Inc./Jodi Jacobson, 16
Seapics.com/James D. Watts, cover, 1, 6
Visuals Unlimited/Reinhard Dirscherl, 20

1 2 3 4 5 6 11 10 09 08 07 06

Table of Contents

Komodo Dragons

In 1910, a Dutch soldier heard stories of monsters on Komodo Island, Indonesia. He went to the tiny island to find them. The soldier didn't find any monsters, but he did find giant lizards. He named them Komodo dragons.

Komodo dragons are a type of monitor lizard. These reptiles can grow quite large. Like other reptiles, monitors have **scales** on their skin and grow from eggs. Reptiles are also **cold-blooded**. They need outside heat to stay warm.

◀ Their large size and sharp claws make Komodo dragons the most dangerous lizards in the world.

What Komodo Dragons Look Like

Komodo dragons are the world's largest lizards. Some are 10 feet (3 meters) long. They weigh as much as 300 pounds (136 kilograms). These giants walk on four short legs with large claws.

A Komodo dragon's skin droops off its body. Most Komodo dragons are black, brown, green, or gray in color. Some have white or yellow patches on their skin.

Each Komodo dragon has about 60 sharp, jagged teeth. The teeth are pointed to tear into **prey**.

◀ Tough, thick skin protects Komodo dragons like armor.

Komodo Dragon Range Map

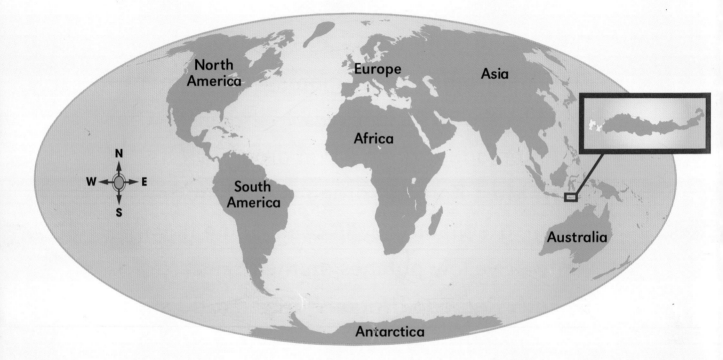

 Where Komodo Dragons Live

Komodo Dragons in the World

Komodo dragons are **endangered**. Very few of them are left in the world.

Most Komodo dragons are found on the island of Komodo. They also live on small nearby islands. Some Komodo dragons swim between islands. Scientists believe 3,000 to 6,000 Komodo dragons live in this area.

Another 200 Komodo dragons are kept in zoos around the world. More young Komodo dragons are raised in zoos each year.

Komodo Dragon Habitats

Rough, hot islands are home to Komodo dragons. Rocky, hilly land covers these tiny islands. Most Komodo dragons can be found in grassy areas near water.

To escape the heat, Komodo dragons use their sharp claws to dig deep **burrows**. Burrows help Komodo dragons keep their bodies at the right temperature.

Adult Komodo dragons live alone. They often claim one area of land as their own. They attack other Komodo dragons they see.

◄ Cool, dark burrows protect Komodo dragons from the hot island climate.

What Komodo Dragons Eat

Adult Komodo dragons eat deer, pigs, goats, cows, and even people. A Komodo dragon hides in tall grass, watching its prey. It attacks when the animal gets close.

A Komodo dragon's mouth is filled with deadly **bacteria**. One bite **infects** its prey. Most animals die soon after being bitten.

Komodo dragons also eat animals that are already dead. They smell dead animals with their long tongues. Komodo dragons can follow the smell for up to 7 miles (11 kilometers).

◄ Komodo dragons use their sharp teeth to tear into large prey, like this water buffalo.

The Life Cycle of a Komodo Dragon

Egg

Hatchling

2-year-old
Komodo
dragon

Adult male
and female

Producing Young

Male Komodo dragons fight each other to win mates. The winner stands on his hind legs to attract a female. The female hisses if she wants the male to leave.

After mating, a female lays 20 to 40 eggs in a nest she digs in the ground. After laying eggs, females leave their nests. The eggs hatch in about eight months.

Komodo dragon hatchlings are tiny. They weigh 2.5 ounces to 3.5 ounces (71 grams to 99 grams). Their green skin is covered with bright yellow stripes.

Growing Up

Few young Komodo dragons live to become adults. Adult Komodos and other **predators** often eat young dragons.

To stay safe, many young Komodo dragons live in trees. They eat insects that crawl along tree branches. They also eat geckos and other small reptiles. Komodos move to the ground when they are about 4 years old and 4 feet (1.2 meters) long.

◄ Young Komodo dragons often live together until they are old enough to fight off predators.

Dangers to Komodo Dragons

People are the biggest danger to Komodo dragons. Hunting Komodo dragons is against the law. But people still kill Komodo dragons. Others destroy Komodo dragon habitats.

Some tourists feed wild Komodo dragons. The reptiles don't learn to hunt, and then they starve when tourists leave.

Most Komodo dragons live in protected areas. Komodo and other islands are part of Komodo National Park. Protecting Komodo dragon habitats will help keep this giant reptile in the world.

◄ Tourists travel to Komodo National Park to watch and photograph the Komodo dragons.

Amazing Facts about Komodos

- Komodo dragons often break their teeth while biting prey. They can grow back up to 200 teeth in a year.
- Komodo dragons can eat half their body weight in food in less than 20 minutes.
- Komodo dragons are fast. They can sprint up to 12 miles (19 kilometers) per hour.
- Komodo dragons can live up to 50 years.
- Scientists believe Komodo dragons are related to a type of lizard that lived 100 million years ago.

◄ Komodo dragons can open their jaws wide enough to swallow whole chunks of food.

Glossary

bacteria (back-TIHR-ee-uh)—tiny organisms that exist inside and around all living things; bacteria can cause diseases.

burrow (BUR-oh)—a tunnel or hole in the ground made or used by an animal

cold-blooded (KOHLD–BLUHD-id)—having a body temperature that is the same as the surroundings; all reptiles are cold-blooded.

endangered (en-DAYN-jurd)—at risk of dying out

infect (in-FEKT)—to cause disease by introducing germs

predator (PRED-uh-tur)—an animal that hunts other animals for food

prey (PRAY)—an animal hunted by another animal for food

scale (SKALE)—one of the small, hard plates that covers the body of a fish or reptile

Read More

Dragon. Animals of the World.
, 2003.

jered Komodo Dragons. Earth's
s. New York: Crabtree, 2005.

n way to
o this book.
nd have been

m

e

-appropriate sites. Or enter a search
ok for a more general search.

outton.

best sites for you!

Index